2008

To D,
at Solidarity, with "best wishes!"
Mary J Mulhern

MW00906178

WHEN ANGELS WEEP

When Angels Weep

Mary Ann Mulhern

Black Moss Press

2008

©Mary Ann Mulhern 2008

Library and Archives Canada Cataloguing in Publication

Mulhern, Mary Ann
    When angels weep / Mary Ann Mulhern.

Poems.
ISBN 978-0-88753-445-4

1. Sexual abuse victims--Poetry. I. Title.

PS8576.U415W44 2008   C811'.6   C2008-901368-9

Cover Design: Katie West

Published by Black Moss Press, 2450 Byng Road, Windsor, Ontario N8W 3E8.
Black Moss Press books are distributed by LitDistco, and all orders should be
directed there.

Black Moss acknowledges the generous support for its publishing program from
The Canada Council for the Arts and The Ontario Arts Council.

Poems from When Angels Weep have been published in Descant's January 2008
edition and www.blueskipoetry.com, which published "Witness in the Dark".

The Canada Council | Le Conseil des Arts
for the Arts | du Canada

ONTARIO ARTS COUNCIL
CONSEIL DES ARTS DE L'ONTARIO

Sexual violation turns all children into the same child. 'Come here. Yes, you.' Children heal quickly, so that, like a tree growing up around an axe, the child grows up healthy until, with time, the embedded thing begins to rust and seep and the idea of extracting it is worse than the thought of dying from it slowly. 'I'm not hurting you.' Once pleasure and poison have entwined, how to separate them? What alchemist, what priest or therapist, what pal or lover?

Ann-Marie MacDonald, *The Way the Crow Flies*

In the Chatham courthouse on August 3, 2006, Father Charles Sylvestre pleaded guilty to forty-seven counts of child sexual abuse, crimes committed over a period of forty years in the Diocese of London, Ontario, Canada.

He abused little girls as young as nine years old in parishes in Windsor, Chatham, Sarnia and London. Bishops moved him to a new parish whenever there were reports of abuse. In some instances, police did not believe the accounts. Frequently parents and teachers accused the girls of lies, sometimes punishing them.

The diocese was not forthcoming with young women who disclosed what had happened to them as children. Only when a gag order was lifted from one of the survivors did this case come to trial. The prosecutor was the Crown Attorney, Paul Bailey. Forty-seven known survivors gave impact statements and listened in a crowded courtroom, as Father Charles Sylvestre pleaded guilty to each and every count.

Sylvestre was sentenced to three years in prison, as he was old and frail. After three months, Charles Sylvestre died in a prison hospital. He seemed incapable of comprehending his legacy of damage. Since the trial, several women have come forward. Some never will.

Bishop Ronald Fabbro made a formal apology to the survivors on Pentecost Sunday at St. Ursula's Church, in Chatham, Ontario. A critical goal of the survivors is prevention. A committee, *From Isolation to Action*, has been formed to draft a policy for the London Diocese.

Poems in "When Angels Weep" are loosely based on survivor accounts and court records. They are intended to allow the survivors a unique expression of their story, their truth.

"I learned that sometimes we enter art to hide within it. It is where we can go to save ourselves, where a third-person voice protects us."

Michael Ondaatje, *Divisadero*

Acknowledgments

I wish to acknowledge Marty Gervais, who believed this book must be written. Also, Paul Bailey, the Crown Attorney who prosecuted the Sylvestre case, has been a remarkable source of information, encouragement and advice.

Four of the survivors met with me and gave me extremely moving and compelling accounts of what had happened to them when they were little girls. I will always be deeply grateful for the courage and generosity of these women.

I wish also to include Penny-Anne Beaudoin, who read many of these poems and suggested edits. Indeed, I was greatly supported in this endeavour by family and friends.

Black Moss Press would like to thank the talented editorial and publishing teams involved in the production of this book. Their labour has been invaluable in every respect. These include: Emily Beaton, Mandy Boreskie, Anne-Marie Charron, Michael Cox, Bill Delisle, Jasmine Elliott, Ashley Girty, Kate Hargreaves, Lindsey Hindi, William Hull, Deni Kasa, Ksenija Kulaib, Donna Luangmany, Neda Marin, Janine Morris, Cristina Naccarato, Crystal Rose Patterson, Danielle Romanello, Melissa Schnarr-Rice, Michal Tellos, and Katie West.

It is my sincere wish that these poems allow the survivors another voice, another channel by which they will be heard.

TABLE OF CONTENTS

for survivors of the Father Charles
Sylvestre abuse case, and for all those
who have survived sexual abuse

When Angels Weep

in a crowded courtroom
an aging priest
stands before a judge
hears forty-seven counts
of sexual abuse
forty-seven women
ghosts of little girls
witness his response
guilty
one word rescued
from the ruin of childhood
recorded in broken lines
of hearts
deep trace of tears

like a blinded eye
the skylight darkens
rain thunders on glass
a lawyer whispers
to his partner
angels have gathered here
to weep

MARY ANN MULHERN

NINE-YEAR-OLD GIRLS

to the prosecutor
the priest blamed
nine-year-old girls
after all, it was
the short skirts they wore
to school
how they sat on chairs
long dangle of legs
their mouths open
to receive communion
pink tongues
soft and moist

CAN'T BE RIGHT

in the rectory
it's a party
chocolate bars and pop
loud music
the Beatles
Maxwell's Silver Hammer
One Tin Soldier
Stay Awhile
two classmates
fold Sunday bulletins
at the oak table
in the hall
Father Charlie lifts me
onto his lap
in his big black chair
beneath a window
with red velvet drapes
he says he'll be my favourite uncle
that I'm special
he points to his cheek
a kiss
points to his lips
a kiss
points to his tongue

MARY ANN MULHERN

I try to move away
his arms become a trap
hands move
under my blouse
beneath my skirt
inside where it
doesn't feel right
can't be right
must be right

he's Father

SWEET PAYMENT

he gives me
chocolate, red and green peppermint
pop with bubbles and froth
sweetness to cover
the bitter taste
food to fill
graveyards of grief
soda and sugared candy
I want to throw up
in dark washroom pails
garbage

MARY ANN MULHERN

ALTAR GIRLS

Father Charlie
teaches us how
to serve weekday mass
to bring water
and a white linen cloth
for the lavabo
washing of hands
purification from sin

on Sundays
we are secrets
clothed in vestments
green purple white black and gold
colours of seasons
advent and lent
birth death resurrection

we are lambs
silent and small
the perfect sacrifice

Mea Culpa

the teacher
prepares us for confession
examination of conscience
disobedience, theft
impure thoughts
impure touches
sins in God's perfect ledger
recorded by angels
numbered by name

behind a dusty velvet curtain
I kneel before a screen
the priest's familiar voice
whispers
secrets I must keep
penance I must make
a litany of lies
to confound any angel
who tries to count

Mary Ann Mulhern

In Nomini Patris

near the back
of St. Ursula's Church
I kneel between my parents
they do not believe
their own flesh and blood
is consumed
by the man
who raises consecrated hands
above the altar
in nomini patris
et filii
et spiritus sanctus
my parents whisper amen

silence turns to stone
like the eyes and ears
of angels and saints
who will not see
will not hear

THIRD EYE

his camera
is a third eye
all seeing, all knowing
black and white
images of me
at my desk
in the playground
at the rectory
folding bulletins
at the oak table
in the bowling alley
poised to bowl
my white panties
showing

he shows slides
to the whole school
I've been enlarged
every pore opened
he smiles before the last slide
looks at me
all the boys
in grade eight
pointing

MARY ANN MULHERN

PROMISE OF HELL

in sleep
I feel myself falling
into flames
my mother
my father
my little brother
beside me
their awful screams
will never end
unless I keep silent
never let words
gather in my throat
whisper in my breath
Father Sylvestre's voice
fills the dark
if you ever say things
if you ever speak

I've been in hell
since grade four
the devil walked
into my classroom
smiled at me

If Jesus Comes Down

I'm in the hold
of Sylvestre's black leather chair
he points to a crucifix
hung high on the painted wall
whispers into my ear
if you ever tell anyone
Jesus will come down
from the cross
and kill you

the crucifix above me
is transformed
suspended in my mind
dark eyes of a wounded God
follow me home
keep vigil at our table
in every room

I remain silent
my mouth dry
lips parched
throat sore
as if words will explode
into darkness
and Jesus will knock
at the door

Mary Ann Mulhern

A Child's Prayer

my angel
departed long ago
flew to a graveyard
where she stands
beside a tombstone
folds her hands
over a holy book
angel of God
my guardian dear
to whom God's love
commits me here

stone eyes turn away
from a child
who follows a priest
into a rectory room
ever this day
be at my side
to light and guard
to rule and guide

I'm in a place
hidden
from the sight
of angels

Somewhere Safe

at home
I tell no one
my closet is
a refuge
skirts, blouses and dresses
neat hangers
all in a row
enough clean cloth
to cover me

my closet is the darkness
I need
the tight corner
where I can curl
into silence
a rag doll
who cries
herself to sleep

Mary Ann Mulhern

BLESS ME FATHER

a door swings shut
in the dark
Father Charlie raises his hand
in a blessing
he says our time
in the confessional is special
commands me to undress
climb into his lap

this secret sacrament
robs my soul of grace
tears the white lace garment
of baptism into rags

when I leave
my clothes feel heavy
wrinkled, unclean
a statue of the virgin
stares down at me
holy Mary
mother of God
pray for us sinners
now, and in the hour
of death

HOW HE REMAINS

a new St. Ursula's
begins to rise
from stones
of the old

Father Charlie
leads my friend and me
through the chaos of construction
tells us
to gather pop bottles
left behind by workers
to redeem them
for a nickel each
afterwards we visit
with him,
leave with candy bars
and soda pop

now when I enter
St. Ursula's church
I feel Sylvestre's presence
his refusal to vanish
his eyes look down

MARY ANN MULHERN

from grey walls
his voice whispers
from throats of sculpted saints

you are my favourite
why don't you
come to visit me anymore?

Recess At St. Ursula's

in grade seven
the playground fence
encircles me
Sylvestre follows
shadows of my fear
like an animal
he attacks from behind
his hands
bruise my breasts
my heart

who would believe
a grade-seven girl
who reports
a monster in the yard
one who wears a white collar
carries rosary beads

Mary Ann Mulhern

To Save Her

my little sister
tells my parents
Father Sylvestre
took her picture
she plans to ride
her bicycle over
to the rectory

in that moment
I see her
in a leather chair
his hands under
her clothes
leaving prints
heavy red and raw
shame she'll never cleanse
never heal
I begin to cry
my screams echo
don't let her go
don't let her go

ILLUSIONS OF MY CHILDHOOD

a priest
visits our house
speaks to my parents
about Sylvestre

he looks at me
my hair shiny and clean
pink cheeks, clear skin
a new dress
white shoes

the priest's eyes
create a lovely illusion
of my childhood
well-mannered, hands held still
only a few, soft words
escape cages of memory
my heart turned
inside out

he tells my parents
your daughter looks fine
no need to say anything
to the bishop
the police

MARY ANN MULHERN

Ego Te Absolvo

Father Sylvestre
ministered
to the sick and dying
his consecrated hands
anointed
eyes ears nose mouth and tongue
holy oils, holy words
ego te absolvo

he washed fingers and palms
visited a classroom
asked for a girl by name
took her to the rectory
for anointment
his hands reached under her dress
white cotton panties
his hands making her sick
his words making her die

FRESH KILL

Father Charlie comes into the playground
black camera around his neck
like a dead bird
fresh kill

he keeps a collection
photos of girls like me
trophies he can display
in all the dark rooms
of his mind

the priest tries to hold me
in the small red eye
open, alive
I turn away
pull my coat
over my face

A Room Upstairs

on the way back
from a Sunday farm
horse rides, apple blooms
ice-cream and lemon cake
I fall asleep
in Father Charlie's car
at the rectory
he carries me upstairs
unlocks a door
a white bed floats
in dark centers of his room
I hear murmurs of water
his shower
his lavabo
a preparation

he appears beside the bed
naked
kisses me, fondles my breasts
begins to bring his body down
on mine
fear explodes in my blood
the crucifix above
illumines a corpse
an angel
an unknown saint

helps me escape
from the bed
from the house
the priest
shadows of a cross
tug at me
at every turn

MARY ANN MULHERN

About A Holy Priest

I tell a friend
whose big sister reports
police come to our door
question me about Father Sylvestre
my mother turns away
from my many tears
I've disgraced her
before neighbours
before the parish

within days
Father leaves
I am blamed
condemned to a closet
at school
the bad little girl
who mouthed filthy lies
about a holy priest

Without My Mother

the day the police
came to our house
my mother left me
on slippery steps of a church
warm membrane of her love
broken
I became an orphan
no hope of grace
redemption from shame

if only I
had been her sacrament
body and blood
from the chalice
of her womb
the rosary she held
in her hands
every bead a prayer
ending in a silvered cross
the one she kissed

MARY ANN MULHERN

At The Beach

I stay in cool water
feel it nestle my body
hide me
from what's going on
beneath a gaudy umbrella
Sylvestre in a small
circle of girls
his pants unzipped
invitation of touch

I know he'll wait
for me
even if light leaves
every wave that reaches shore
fingers curled against harm
my hands will shake

afterwards I will
rub sand into my palms
until there is blood
enough to wash away
the smell

SEAL OF CONFESSION

did he confess
to a fellow priest
tell what he did
with little girls
their lives
a purple penitence
their bodies
breathing temptation
into the flesh and blood
of his consecrated hands

were the words
of absolution magic
enough to cleanse his soul
to give permission
for this week's visit
to a grade four class

MARY ANN MULHERN

Naptime With Father Charlie

in my dream
a little girl
lies on a bed
a holy bible
rests on a small table
the child cries
for help

I am the little girl
in Father Charlie's bed
he says it's naptime
at first his touches
only tickle
until suddenly
his weight smothers me
pain breaks
my body open
a wound bleeds
the bible blurs
all upside down

at night
I'm afraid to sleep
afraid of blood
ruin of white
nightgown and sheets

dark, wet spots
widen into eyes
they will watch
me die
slow haze of red
unless I stay awake
unless I stay
awake

MAGDALENE

in the rectory
I help with an Easter banner
white lilies on linen
purple letters that sing
alleluia

a housekeeper serves tea
Father pours liquor
into his painted cup
his hands reach
under my clothes
between my legs
he says
I'm Mary Magdalene
with my many sins

I will never be saved
I have no alabaster jar
ointment to soothe
tears to wash the feet of Jesus
hair long enough
to wipe them dry

In The Playground

little kids
run to Father Charlie
grab his hands
hang onto his arms

I huddle in a corner
with some older girls
they warn me
to button my coat
to the neck
to cross my arms
over my breasts
they say
he'll get inside your coat
stay away
from his hands

Mary Ann Mulhern

THREE LETTERS OF SEX

in grade six
three letters
slam together
thunder in my flesh
my bones
sex
is what the priest
is doing to me
in the black lap
of his leather chair

God
did not gather me
into the shelter
of his arms
did not strike
Sylvestre down
he's picked me
for his hell

ROADS TO HELL AND HEALING

grade seven - marijuana
grade eight - marijuana and alcohol
grade nine - marijuana and needles
grade ten - marijuana and needles and sex

I had to be
high or drunk
or both
to have sex
to kill the smell
of Sylvestre
boozy rye
cheap after-shave
rubbed against my skin
without the wild inhale of pot
I would have gone mad
taken all the drugs
cut every vein

MARY ANN MULHERN

MIRROR MIRROR

my ten-year-old body
looks out from a mirror
small frame of bones
covered with flesh
a homemade cotton dress
conceals nothing
I can see
the bad little girl inside
she's the one
who's real
she wants the mirror
to turn into water
clear and deep
enough for me to sink
into darkness

my image
dissolves into thousands of tiny dots
none of them connected
to who I was
who I might have been

FAREWELL TEA

my mother dresses
for a tea-party
Father Charlie's farewell
long flowered skirt
pearls around her throat
he gives her a signed photo
of himself
says it's for me
a very special
little girl

my mother is an ex-nun
white veil of faith
pulled tight against my words
a chair in the rectory
hands under my clothes
she abandons me
in the silence
of her cloister
never speak of this
to your father
to anyone

TEST FOR CONFIRMATION

I follow Father Charlie
to a room down the hall
he'll test me
before confirmation

I am told to
take off my panties
sit in his lap
my body is the temple
of the Holy Spirit
the priest's hands destroy
every sacred gift
wisdom
understanding
knowledge
piety
fortitude
counsel
fear of the Lord

I am to blame
I am not worthy
of the sacrament
innocence of white
the bishop's anointment
holy oil of Chrism

signed in a cross
sacred on my skin

I am to blame
he tells me

To Bury Memory

on the way back
to the classroom
I force myself
to bury shame
every shadow of memory
his smell, sin all over me
I will erase this
like chalk on a board
until there is only dust
dark particles
swept into hidden corners
silent and sealed
forbidden to shape thoughts
or words

it never happened
the room doesn't exist
there is no chair
no priest

WITNESS IN THE DARK

my grandfather's face
sinks into red hollows
he snarls I'm a liar
makes me wash
in the claw foot tub
drives me back
to St. Ursula's
leaves me
with Father Sylvestre
to confess

statues of saints
watch from pedestals
witness what happens
so does the Madonna
she must hear my cries
yet when I look up
nothing has changed
she still holds her child
leaves me alone
with the priest

MARY ANN MULHERN

CLASSROOM CLOSET

in religion class
I begin to weep
Sister Mary Basil
takes me into the hall
asks what's wrong
I tell her
what Father
does to me
at the rectory
her lips tighten
into a straight line
liar, she hisses
dirty, disgusting little girl

the nun orders me
into a closet
at the back of the room
I walk between rows
of silent classmates
other girls who know

coats damp
with morning rain
hang from hooks
like garments worn by ghosts

long sleeves
fill with arms and hands
that reach out
to strangle me

Thirty Years Later

I can't be alone
in the night
my husband calls
says he has to work
until dawn
tells me to phone my mother
before the dream begins
I switch on all the lights
the house becomes a closet
with no latch
Father Sylvestre and Sister Mary Basil laugh
heavy coats
swing from hooks
swarm around my head
all of them black
as a nun's habit
a priest's cassock
rosary beads
rattle like snakes
ready to strike

Sunday Dinner

Father Charlie
sometimes says mass
in our house
stays for dinner
takes his place
next to me
at the oak table

he teases
about my piece
of chocolate cake
asks if I want to trade

my mother smiles
says he would
have made
a great dad

SATAN'S CLAIM

hidden in a hooded cape
Satan appears
in my dream
I raise my hand
in the sign
of the cross
he grabs my arm
asks who I am
I whisper my name
he laughs
low, mean chuckle
like Father Sylvestre
I know who you are
when you call
the Great One
he will not be there
for you

the devil claims me
a dirty little girl
who deserves hell
I smell my fear
rye, cheap aftershave
an old man

Before And After

before Sylvestre's hands
silenced my song
I played guitar
hummed folksy tunes
took jazz and ballet
my body shaped
to music
an instrument of grace
lovely as Giselle
or Juliette

in my teens
I disappeared
from every stage
searched for safety
in corners of my room
a quiet girl
who read Shakespeare
Hamlet, Othello, Lear

my mother didn't know
couldn't know
why

MARY ANN MULHERN

When The Camera Lies

Father stands
on the steps of a church
flashes an Easter morning smile

in the April breeze
priestly vestments billow
into angel wings
illusion of fabric
puff of wind

I see the man
who hurts me
my mother sees a parish priest
hears him chant
alleluia, alleluia, alleluia

SACRILEGE

on the way home
from skating
a door swings open
Father Charlie offers a ride
within moments he stops
pulls up my sweater, my skirt
grabs at my breasts
gropes between my legs
sacrilege of trust

my mother sees my face
my clothes, my hair
she believes me
yet my father scorns me
as a disgrace, a liar
with his words
he invokes darkness
a legacy of loss
disappearance of God
every vestige
of a father's love

MARY ANN MULHERN

Looking For Me

why was Sylvestre
driving on my street
in his black funeral car
was he looking
for me
did he recognize me
as a bad girl
something he'd noticed
in a photo from school
brightness in my eyes
long hair left untied
sleeveless blouse, short skirt
evidence misread
from my confessions
sins stored like
dark coins he loved
to count
enough to bargain
I would be willing
the kind of girl
he could pick up
easily

Rye And Coke

at a high school party
someone offers
rye and coke
in a thick-bottomed glass
slow melt of ice

the drink in my hand
bubbles poison
that breaks into sweat
over my face and breasts

a familiar smell
of Father Sylvestre
of the rectory
rye crushed from summer grain
swells inside of me
until the glass breaks
all the pieces stained
enough for windows
in a church
angels smiling down

Mary Ann Mulhern

THE ABORTION

I'm fifteen
sick every day
something swells
beneath my skirt
my bra
a doctor says I'll sleep
while he scrapes
my womb

this came from Sylvestre
dark foetus of sin
I am the devil-child
the one my grandfather
drives home
pale reflection in glass
sudden blur of snow
no words
only a scar
slow seep of blood

I want to vanish
in the blizzard
cover myself
in white

Shadow Girl

Sylvestre's eyes and hands
have shaped me
into a shadow girl
who hides under
faded shirts – extra large
rain coats buttoned high
granny dresses pleated wide
glasses tinted dark

I'll never know
the girl who lived before
if she can still breathe
beneath all these layers
heavy on my chest
wrapped tight around my legs
enough to drag me away
from every dance

Mary Ann Mulhern

Old Enough To Leave

I'm sixteen
a ghost in the house
of childhood
my parents have become
angry shadows
outside my room
at the table
I eat bread with no butter
never touch meat
it helps me
feel invisible

in the fall
I disappear
on a bus
my mother removes
the extra chair
she knows
I won't return
for Christmas
I've gone too far

CREEPING CHARLIE

last fall
I dug up my garden
ripped out roots
of the purple predator
creeping Charlie

over the winter
it went underground
hid like Charles Sylvestre
under vestments of white

this spring
it spreads over my lawn
weaves a dark scapular
like the one the priest
wore around his neck
when he made me
confess

MARY ANN MULHERN

Wedding Photo

May 21, 1983

I stand at the altar
between my husband
and the priest
vows have been made
until death

threads of fear
whisper along the seams
of all this satin and lace
there is a pen
in my hand
Father Sylvestre points
to where I must sign
who would notice
the angle of my shoulder
turned away
grip of my fingers
curled against
even a glance
the slightest touch

First Communion

my daughter prepares
for first communion
white dress
white veil
white shoes
a priest asks
if he can speak
to my child
alone

his collar
chokes my words
brings back
a little girl
in a rectory chair
beneath a window
with red velvet drapes
every ray of sun
turned to black

why do I
feel guilty even now
saying no
to a priest

Mary Ann Mulhern

69

CLERICAL COLLAR

when I'm thirty-one
I meet with a priest
from the sexual abuse committee
he shows me to a small room
in the rectory
closes the door

his starched collar begins
to encircle me
press around my chest
with the strength of arms

I shrink back
unable to remove my coat
become a ten-year-old child
who has no words
only the brine of tears
to dissolve dark crystals
of memory
so carefully preserved
from these harsh splinters
of light

SMALL AD IN CLASSIFIEDS

in the early nineties
I place a small ad
in papers
Windsor, London, Chatham, Sarnia

Do you remember Father Charles Sylvestre?
Confidentiality guaranteed
Reply box 379

like refugees
from famine, war and drought
letters cross
borders of silence
I am not alone
I never was

a year later
the same ad
is censored
by every paper
the words banned
cancelled
shredded into whispers
no one can read

MARY ANN MULHERN

HIS REAL WIFE

I always wondered why
my husband chose me
why he stayed with me

I had to keep
a marriage veil
in place
exist in small frames
white and black illusion
of the perfect wife
always afraid
of any uncovering
sudden shift of light
where I would be revealed
to my husband
diminished
to the woman
whom I have hidden
from his trusting eyes

If I Hide

there is a space
between me and love
light slips into fog
birds are silent
nothing grows
I know the priest
is there
in his long, black robe
if I hide
he'll find me
if I enter the gap
his scent
will cover my hair
fill pores of my skin
fibres of my clothes

keep better men away

Mary Ann Mulhern

WHILE MY HUSBAND SLEEPS

I awaken
from a dream
black root of memory
shaking, crying
pain between my legs
slow pulse of death
I know he was here
in this room
his hands under
my clothes
probe of his finger
a wound inside of me

in this hour
no one can touch me
my flesh a shell
fragments of my being
held together
in silence
in the dark
like bones in a grave

In The Basement

I never go alone
into the basement
on every step
I see a priest
who leads me down
where memory twists
around my feet, hands and mouth
a jittery bulb
withholds light
Father speaks softly
his voice gentle

I know what happens
between rows of rectory shelves
lined with jars
apples, pears, peaches and plums
ripe colours of sun
picked by
fingers and palms
peeled
devoured to the core
thrown away

MARY ANN MULHERN

What's Wrong?

my husband
brings home a friend
a man from work
when he shakes my hand
I smell Sylvestre
my instincts raw
sharp as any animal
in the wild
scent of rye
poison in my mouth

I scream at my husband
to get this man out
of the house
before Sylvestre creeps in
his hands over the light
darkness in every room
a white collar
coiled on a chair

Hand In Marriage

my first husband
knew I was not a virgin
before our wedding night

he says I've cheated him
of his right
his marriage claim

down the street
there's a thirteen-year-old
showing off her breasts
tight mini-skirts
long Lolita hair

my husband
takes her for a ride
tells her lies
has his virgin child

I'm wearing a wedding ring
when I closed my eyes
Charles Sylvestre
placed it on my hand

MARY ANN MULHERN

77

COLLISION

at midnight
I sometimes race
a train
the engine of my car
strains against the weight
of speed
an uneven match
like a priest
and an eleven-year-old child

I died in that collision
but I continue
to breathe
a condition
often confused
with life

DEFROCKED

at the police station
Sylvestre wears a grey shirt
short sleeved
no roman collar
his shoulders stooped
hair stringy and grey
ordinary

an officer presses him
questions about little girls
sexual offences
the priest sneers
what do you want me to do
break down, cry
say I did it ?

For The First Time

seminarians
form a group
during my talk
I tell them
that if a woman
ever speaks
of a priest
who abuses her
never to bring
her to a small room
in a rectory
close the door
wear a white collar

the priest
who teaches them
reaches for his collar
removes it from my sight
I feel a knotted rope
slip from my throat

for the first time
someone in the church
has heard me

WHERE ARE THEY?

where are all the photos
he took
little girls
in his big chair
on the couch
all in a row
dolls in a store
big eyes, long lashes, curly hair, pink lips
short dresses, white socks
shoes with perfect bows

he kept the negatives
shiny and black
so he could make copies
paste them
into a book
bring us all back
touch us again
smile

MARY ANN MULHERN

To A Young Detective

if a woman says
something happened
years ago
when she was nine
a priest
whose hands
took away her life

don't ask
why didn't you tell
your mother
your teacher
your principal

who would believe
her then
when you
question her now?

GOOD OLD CHARLIE

after the trial
a priest tells me
he lived in a rectory
with Charles Sylvestre
little girls every day
boxes of candy bars
bottles of rye
opened before noon
the house whispered secrets
in the dark
names of little girls
a litany of loss

his bishop only laughed
no worry there
good old Charlie

MARY ANN MULHERN

In The Editor's Box

a letter appears
in the *Windsor Star*
written by a woman
who says
enough
has been smeared
on the front page
about pedophile priests

she says the priests are gone
the abuse is past
her words
a whiteout of wrong

a victim writes back
her pain
alive on the page
priests who continue
to abuse
now

From My Sister

outside the Chatham courthouse
my younger sister
hands me a letter
she writes of a day
twenty years ago
when I screamed
at our parents
not to let her go
to Sylvestre
to the shame
of his hands
she thanks me now
her writing round and clear
she says I saved her
loved her enough
to tell
to risk myself
for my sister

MARY ANN MULHERN

My Father's Peace

days before the end
my father speaks
of Charles Sylvestre
Daddy, I was one
of those little girls
my words break
whispers of his rosary
honey, why didn't you
ever tell me?

forgive us our trespasses
as we forgive
the worn beads slip
from my father's hands
the priest robs him
robs me again
in this small room
my father struggles
for breath
my name caught
in his throat
his prayers lost
murmurs in the dark

From Cemetery Stones

forty-seven of us
gather in a courtroom
a priest in a white collar
pleads forty-seven times
guilty, guilty, guilty
there are empty chairs
of women
who listen from graves

I feel their presence
whispers of names
from cemetery stones
that remember
and weep

STEEL DOOR

in the courtroom
Sylvestre hands
the Crown Attorney
a book on forgiveness
he says the women
must understand
must forgive

he is handcuffed
led to a steel door
entrance to a long tunnel
his prison cell
the heavy door clangs
behind the priest
like a dark note
in a church
or a theatre
sound rises to nine skylights
in the high ceiling
witness of a sudden storm
forty-seven survivors wait
for the last
hollow tone

their first breath

MARY ANN MULHERN

Mary Ann Mulhern, author of *Touch the Dead* and *The Red Dress*, grew up as a gravedigger's daughter in St. Thomas, Ontario. Commissioned to write *When Angels Weep*, Mary Ann faced one of the greatest challenges of her writing career. Having spent seven years in a convent as an aspiring nun, she became familiar with the secrets and beliefs surrounding the Catholic Church. It would only be appropriate that someone so well-acquainted with the inner aspects of the Catholic faith were to write on one of the most controversial topics surrounding the religion today. Channeling the voices of the women who were victimized by Father Charles Sylvestre, Mary Ann has been identified as the perfect voice to relay their story.

Marquis Book Printing Inc.

Québec, Canada
2008